MW01165584

Bible Story Skitlets Too

By Sandra Collier

Illustrated by Jean Bruns

CPH

SAINT LOUIS

For John and Julia.

Copyright © 1999 Concordia Publishing House
3558 S. Jefferson Avenue, St. Louis, MO 63118-3968
Manufactured in the United States of America

Educational institutions or teachers who purchase this product may reproduce pages for classroom use or for use in parish-education programs.

1   2   3   4   5   6   7   8   9   10   07   06   05   04   03   02   01   00   99

Contents

Introduction

Get Ready!

The ten skitlets in *Bible Story Skitlets Too* are designed to be led by a narrator. The narrator guides the children through each 5- to 10-minute reenactment of a Bible story, prompting simple, repeat-after-me lines of dialogue, directing children's movements, and cuing sound effects. Each skitlet has also been designed so that *every* class member is an integral player in the reenactment.

Six Steps to a Successful Performance

1. Recruit another adult to help coordinate the children's movements.
2. Make photocopies of the skitlet for yourself and your helper.
3. Read through the skitlet twice—read it aloud at least once. Seek natural pauses in the repeat-after-me lines so the child (or children) repeating them doesn't stumble or falter.
4. Photocopy the number of masks and accessories suggested for the skitlet in the **Costumes and Props** section. Assemble them as directed. If you would like to photocopy a mask for each child to wear during the skitlet, be careful to follow the directions within the skitlet that are for the masked character roles only. Make sure the individual character portrayals are distinct so the narrative flows and is coherent.
5. Gather the suggested props. Most props can be found in the classroom, but feel free to get creative.
6. Gather from your **Skit Kit** (suggested components are below) those items that would further enhance the performance. The **Skit Kit** is a wonderful way to really dress up the skitlet. Have each child in class wear something from the **Skit Kit** so he or she feels more involved in the reenactment.

Classroom Skit Kit

Gather the items listed below—suggested costume elements and props—and store them in a large box in your classroom. Have your class help you decorate the outside of the box and label it **The Skit Kit**. The items in your **Skit Kit** will add to the fun, so be creative!

- Costume jewelry, bead necklaces, rings, and bracelets
- Five or six X-large men's T-shirts in earth tones (for use as robes)
- Several rulers and yardsticks (for use as walking staffs and sceptres)
- Several small- to medium-sized boxes
- Several 1-yard squares of cloth (for use as head coverings or wraps)
- Women's hair scrunchies (to use as headbands to hold head covering in place)
- Five or six women's scarves in earth tones (for use as belts and sashes)
- Laminated copies of the masks and accessories so they're always available. The initial expense of laminating masks and accessories will be offset by the time you will save. Having them readily available will also give you the opportunity to be spontaneous. With certain skitlets or for a small class, you may want to photocopy masks and let each child decorate his or her own.

Get Set!

The Skitlet Format

Casting Call

This section tells you what masked roles need to be assigned. It also lists supporting players who do not have to be masked but who need to be ready during the performance. Try not to assign the masked roles or the speaking parts only to children with outgoing personalities. In fact, the masked roles would be perfect for the more reserved children in your class—the masks may help them feel less self-conscious.

If your class is small, you may want individual children to portray multiple roles. Performing some of the skitlets with fewer than eight children will be challenging but not impossible. Be creative and have fun.

Costumes and Props

This section tells you the number of specific masks and accessories needed. The face masks have been designed so each one can represent several types of characters, depending upon which accessories are added. Below are examples of basic face masks with various accessories to show the range of possible characters.

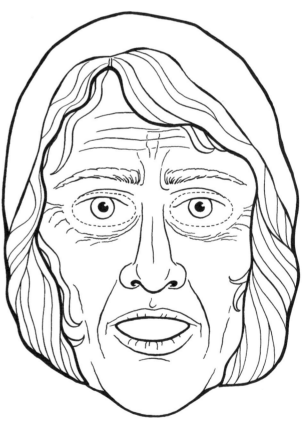

Assembling Masks and Accessories

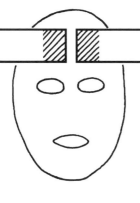

Cut out masks and accessories along heavy outer lines. Cut out eye and mouth holes in the masks. Glue strips of poster board or laminated paper to the back of the masks, as shown in illustration.

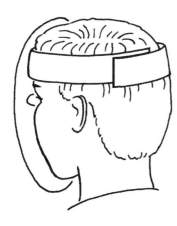

Use self-adhesive Velcro brand fasteners (available at craft and sewing stores) to adjust the mask to fit the child's head. Use the same fasteners to attach accessories (hair, crown, etc.) to the masks, or simply tape or glue the pieces in place.

Cut sword handles along dotted lines. Tape or glue sword handle as illustrated.

Setting the Stage

This section tells you how to stage the children to begin each skitlet. This is where you hand out masks, assign roles, and work out an arranged signal for which the children watch or listen. When you give the signal during the skitlet, it will prompt dialogue, necessary movements, or sound effects.

The Skitlet

The words in **boldface** are the repeat-after-me lines. If you are working with very young children who may not be able to repeat all the lines, have them use gestures to "act out" what you are saying. The *italicized* directions (indicated by the theater mask symbols) are the movements and spacing for the children. The spacing has been determined based upon a standard-sized classroom. Modify the movements and spacing for your classroom or meeting area. Character names are in capital letters in the stage directions so they are easily identified. In **Setting the Stage** and in the stage directions within each skitlet, pronouns generally reflect the gender of the character. Please feel free to have children of either gender play any character. Remember, the important thing is to get your students involved in telling the story and to have fun.

Go!

Now you're ready to take your class in a new direction. Don't worry about a flawless performance—if you have fun with the skitlets, the children will too. Structure the skitlets so your class will have both fun and a wonderful learning opportunity!

Miriam and Aaron's Pride

Numbers 12

Casting Call:
4 Characters + Class

Masked Roles: Moses, Aaron, and Miriam

Supporting Players: Pillar of Cloud and Israelites

Costumes and Props:

You will need:

Moses: mask 1 and accessory 3

Aaron: mask 1 and accessories 4 and 6

Miriam: mask 3 and accessory 2

Setting the Stage:

MOSES stands in front of AARON and MIRIAM on one side of the room. The rest of the children are ISRAELITES; they stand behind AARON and MIRIAM.

Count	Item
2	Mask 1
1	Mask 2
	Mask 3
	Mask 4
1	Accessory 1
1	Accessory 2
1	Accessory 3
	Accessory 4
1	Accessory 5
	Accessory 6
	Accessory 7
	Accessory 8
	Accessory 9
	Accessory 10
	Accessory 11
	Accessory 12
	Accessory 13
	Accessory 14
	Accessory 15
	Accessory 16

NARRATOR: God chose Moses to lead the Israelites out of Egypt, where they had been slaves.

MOSES leads AARON, MIRIAM, and ISRAELITES to the center of the room. ISRAELITES say, **"Thank you, Lord, for giving us Moses as our leader."**

NARRATOR: God chose Moses' brother and sister, Aaron and Miriam, to help Moses.

MOSES turns to AARON and says, **"I thank God for you, Aaron. The Lord gave you the words to say to Pharaoh that helped set us free."** *MOSES turns to MIRIAM and says,* **"Miriam, I thank the Lord for you too. Without your encouragement, I would have found it hard to lead our people."**

NARRATOR: But once in the wilderness, Miriam and Aaron were unhappy with just helping Moses. They thought they should do less helping and more leading.

ISRAELITES gather around MOSES; MIRIAM and AARON move to one side. ISRAELITES say, **"Moses, what do you think we should do?"** *and* **"You're the only one who can help us."**

NARRATOR: Miriam and Aaron began to feel jealous of Moses' special relationship with the Israelites. Miriam and Aaron asked, **"Has the Lord spoken only through Moses?"**

ISRAELITES gather around MIRIAM and AARON, shake their heads and say, **"No! The Lord has worked through you too."**

NARRATOR: Miriam and Aaron asked, **"Hasn't He also spoken through us?"**

ISRAELITES nod their heads and say, **"Yes! The Lord had Aaron help Moses talk to Pharaoh. And the Lord worked through Miriam when she led the celebration after we escaped from Egypt."**

NARRATOR: Then Miriam and Aaron said the worst thing about Moses. Miriam and Aaron said, **"Moses thinks he doesn't have to follow the same rules we do! He thinks he's better than us."**

ISRAELITES turn to one another and say, **"You know, I think they're right. Maybe we shouldn't let Moses lead us anymore. Maybe we should choose a new leader."** *MOSES kneels where he is standing, as if in prayer.*

NARRATOR: Miriam and Aaron were turning the Israelites against the Lord's chosen servant, Moses, and the Lord grew angry with Miriam and Aaron. The Lord knew that Moses was humble and that Moses relied not on his own strength and wisdom, but on the Lord's.

MOSES says, **"Lord, show me what you want me and my people to do."**

NARRATOR: Moses sought only God's will for everything in his life, and obeyed the Lord with his whole heart. That was why the Lord picked Moses to be the leader of the Israelites.

MOSES stands up and joins MIRIAM and AARON. ISRAELITES form a circle around MOSES, MIRIAM, and AARON.

NARRATOR: Moses, Miriam, and Aaron were in the Tent of Meeting worshiping, when the Lord told them to come outside. Moses, Aaron, and Miriam obeyed the Lord and went outside.

MOSES, MIRIAM, and AARON come stand on the outside of the circle of ISRAELITES.

NARRATOR: Then the Lord presented Himself as a pillar of cloud to Moses, Miriam, and Aaron; He stood at the entrance to the Tent of Meeting so they could not go back inside.

PILLAR OF CLOUD stands between the circle of ISRAELITES and MOSES, MIRIAM, and AARON, and stretches out his or her arms as if blocking MOSES, MIRIAM, and AARON from going back into the circle.

NARRATOR: Then the Lord summoned Aaron and Miriam to stand before Him.

MOSES bows his head. MIRIAM and AARON each take a step toward PILLAR OF CLOUD.

NARRATOR: The Lord said, "Listen to My words. When a prophet of the Lord is among you, I reveal Myself to him in visions, I speak to him in dreams." Miriam and Aaron said, **"But we're Your prophets too! And aren't You revealing Yourself to us in this pillar of cloud?"** The Lord continued, "But with My servant Moses, I speak to him in person so that he sees Me clearly … have I done that with you?"

MIRIAM and AARON shake their heads and say, **"No, Lord. We have never seen You face-to-face as Moses has."**

NARRATOR: The Lord asked Miriam and Aaron, "Why then were you not afraid to speak against My servant Moses?"

MIRIAM and AARON begin shaking and saying, **"But we thought …"** *and* **"We're sorry, Lord, we were only trying to …"**

NARRATOR: But the Lord wouldn't listen to their excuses. He was angry with Miriam and Aaron. When Miriam and Aaron had questioned whether Moses should be their leader, they really were questioning the Lord's decisions.

PILLAR OF CLOUD circles AARON and MIRIAM several times. MOSES raises his head and he and ISRAELITES say, **"What's going to happen to them?"** *PILLAR OF CLOUD rejoins the circle of ISRAELITES.*

NARRATOR: Then the Lord left them and the pillar of cloud lifted from about the tent and there stood Miriam—white as snow.

MOSES, MIRIAM, and AARON go stand in the center of the circle of ISRAELITES again. ISRAELITES say, **"What has happened to Miriam? She has turned whiter than snow."**

NARRATOR: The LORD had marked Miriam with a skin disease so that all who looked at her would know that the LORD was angry with her for disobeying Him. The LORD had punished Miriam on the outside so that all who saw her would know that she had done something wrong. The LORD punished Aaron too, but it was on the inside, where no one could see. The LORD made Aaron's conscience bother him.

AARON puts an arm around MIRIAM's shoulders and says, **"Oh, no! What have we done? Oh LORD, I am so sorry for what we have done."**

NARRATOR: Aaron said to Moses, **"Please do not hold our sin against us because of our foolish pride. Please don't let Miriam suffer with this disease."**

MOSES gets on his knees and raises his hands above his head.

NARRATOR: So Moses cried out to the LORD, **"O God, please heal her!"** The LORD replied to Moses, "Just as she would be punished for disobeying her earthly father, she must still be punished for disobeying Me. Miriam must live apart from all the Israelites for seven days so she has time to think about what she has done wrong."

MOSES and AARON join the circle of ISRAELITES, leaving MIRIAM alone in the middle. Then MOSES, AARON, and ISRAELITES turn their backs on MIRIAM.

NARRATOR: So for seven days, Miriam had to live all by herself with no one to talk to or comfort her.

MOSES, AARON, and ISRAELITES sit down in their places and bow their heads.

NARRATOR: All the other Israelites had to wait to continue on their journey to the Promised Land until Miriam was allowed to rejoin them.

MOSES, AARON, and ISRAELITES stand and face MIRIAM. Then MOSES leads the group to the side of the room.

NARRATOR: After this time of waiting, the Israelites continued their journey to the Promised Land, with Moses, the LORD's chosen servant, leading the way.

By Faith Alone
Judges 6–8

Casting Call:
4 Characters + Class

Masked Roles: Gideon, Angel, and at least two Midianites

Supporting Players: Judges, Israelites

Costumes and Props:

You will need:

Gideon: mask 2 and accessories 3 and 16

Angel: mask 2 and accessory 4

Midianite 1: mask 1 and accessories 3 and 7

Midianite 2: mask 1 and accessories 3 and 9

Israelites: accessory 16 for each member of class

Setting the Stage:

Up to 12 JUDGES, GIDEON, ANGEL, and the MIDIANITES wait by your side. The rest of the class, the ISRAELITES, wait on one side of the room. Keep the horns with you and distribute them as directed within the skitlet.

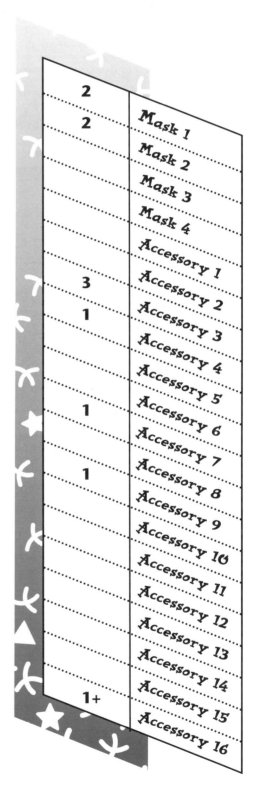

2	Mask 1
2	Mask 2
	Mask 3
	Mask 4
	Accessory 1
3	Accessory 2
1	Accessory 3
	Accessory 4
	Accessory 5
1	Accessory 6
	Accessory 7
1	Accessory 8
	Accessory 9
	Accessory 10
	Accessory 11
	Accessory 12
	Accessory 13
	Accessory 14
1+	Accessory 15
	Accessory 16

NARRATOR: Long ago, the LORD placed a group of wise men and women, one from each of the twelve tribes of Israel, as leaders to guide the Israelites. These leaders were called Judges.

JUDGES go to center of room.

NARRATOR: The judges made decisions about how best to take care of the Israelites and protect the Israelite homeland from other people. Soon the Israelites began to look to these judges as their true rulers, and forgot that their authority and wisdom came from the LORD.

Some of the ISRAELITES go to the JUDGES and say, "Please, help us with our problem." JUDGES ask, "Have you prayed to the LORD about it?" ISRAELITES respond, "No, you can understand our problem better because you're like us." The rest of the ISRAELITES now go surround the JUDGES. All the ISRAELITES say, "The LORD seems so far away and you are right here … you know our needs better than the LORD." JUDGES now become ISRAELITES.

NARRATOR: Because the Israelites had forgotten His ways, God allowed a group of people called the Midianites to conquer Israel and rule over them. It was a very hard time for the Israelites, since their lands and all their belongings were taken by the Midianites.

MIDIANITES approach ISRAELITES and say, "What huge flocks of sheep you have—now they're mine!" and "You and your family will be my servants." MIDIANITES go to one side of the room and sit down.

NARRATOR: But the LORD remembered the special relationship He had with the Israelites. So after seven years of the Midianites ruling Israel, when the Israelites called to the LORD for help, the LORD chose a man named Gideon to be His servant and to set the Israelites free.

GIDEON and ANGEL go stand to one side of the ISRAELITES.

NARRATOR: The LORD sent an angel to Gideon. The angel said, **"The LORD is with you, mighty warrior."** "But sir," Gideon replied, **"If the LORD is with us, why has all this happened to us? The LORD has abandoned us and put us into the hands of Midian."** The angel said, **"Go in the strength that you have and save Israel out of Midian's hand."** **"But how can I save Israel?"** Gideon asked. **"My family is the least important of all the families in the tribe of Manasseh, which is the least important of all the tribes in Israel. And I am the least important in my family."** The angel of the LORD answered, **"The LORD will be with you and help you make all the Midianites leave Israel."** Gideon wasn't sure that the LORD was really talking to him, so he asked the LORD for a sign. The LORD gave Gideon the sign he had asked for, and the angel left.

ANGEL removes mask and becomes one of the ISRAELITES. GIDEON continues to stand alone. Give GIDEON a horn.

NARRATOR: Gideon had faith in the LORD and Gideon did what the LORD told him to do.

GIDEON raises the horn as if blowing it.

NARRATOR: Gideon blew a trumpet to call people to follow him into battle against the Midianites. Men from several of the Israelite tribes joined Gideon.

The ISRAELITES surround GIDEON. ISRAELITES say, "Gideon will lead us to freedom from the Midianites!"

NARRATOR: Eventually the number of men who followed Gideon reached 32,000. But Gideon was still having doubts about what the LORD wanted him to do.

GIDEON walks among the ISRAELITES surrounding him and then stands to one side of the ISRAELITE group. He says, "I wish I could be sure that the LORD will save Israel through me like He said."

NARRATOR: Gideon asked the LORD for another sign. He said to God, **"Look, I will place a wool fleece on the threshing floor. In the morning, if there is dew only on the fleece and all the ground around it is dry, then I will know for sure that You will save Israel through me as You have promised."**

GIDEON acts out placing something on the floor.

NARRATOR: Gideon got up early the next day; the ground around the fleece was dry and the fleece was wet with dew.

GIDEON acts out picking up something from floor and making wringing motions.

NARRATOR: Even with the proof that he'd asked for, Gideon was still unsure. He asked the LORD for yet another sign. Gideon said, **"Don't be angry with me. Let me make just one more request. Allow me one more test with the fleece. This time make the fleece dry in the morning and the ground all around it covered with dew."** The next morning, the fleece was dry while all the ground around it was covered with dew.

GIDEON acts out picking something up off the floor and says, "Now I am sure that the LORD will do as He says." GIDEON and the ISRAELITES move closer to the MIDIANITES.

NARRATOR: Gideon and his army moved closer to where the Midianites were camped. But the LORD said to Gideon, "You have too many men for Me to deliver Midian into their hands. So that all of Israel will know that it is by My power that they are saved from the Midianites, tell your army, "Anyone who trembles with fear may turn back and leave." So 22,000 men left Gideon's army and only 10,000 remained.

Several of the ISRAELITES come stand by you.

NARRATOR: But the LORD said, "There are still too many men." He told Gideon to test his men to see which ones were truly ready to go into battle. Gideon tested his men as the LORD had told him to, and out of 10,000 soldiers, only 300 were to go with Gideon to fight the Midianites. The rest of Gideon's men returned to their tents.

🎭 *The ISRAELITES around GIDEON should stay with him.*

NARRATOR: Gideon had done all that the LORD had asked him to do. While Gideon didn't doubt the LORD, he was still unsure of himself. The LORD knew this and gave Gideon encouragement. The LORD told Gideon to sneak into the Midianite camp that night and listen to what they were saying.

🎭 *GIDEON and one ISRAELITE creep over to the MIDIANITES and then crouch down.*

🎭 *One MIDIANITE says, "Gideon is coming on behalf of his God and we will lose." Have GIDEON and the ISRAELITE return to the rest of the ISRAELITES. Have the children standing by you join them. Hand out trumpets to all the ISRAELITES now.*

NARRATOR: Gideon returned to his army of 300 and told them, **"Get up! The LORD has given the Midianite camp into your hands."** Gideon then split his 300 soldiers into three groups of 100.

🎭 *Divide the ISRAELITES into three groups.*

NARRATOR: All 300 men carried trumpets and torches that were shielded so that no light would show until they were ready.

🎭 *ISRAELITES say, "Why are all of us carrying torches and trumpets? Usually only a few men in an army do."*

NARRATOR: Gideon said, **"Follow me and watch what I do. When I get to the edge of the camp, do exactly as I do."**

🎭 *The three groups of ISRAELITES walk to the MIDIANITES and surround them.*

NARRATOR: Gideon and the Israelites surrounded the Midianites. Gideon and the 100 men with him blew their trumpets and broke the jars that had shielded the light of their torches. The other 200 Israelites did exactly what Gideon did.

🎭 *ISRAELITES pantomime blowing their horns and make trumpeting noises.*

NARRATOR: The Israelites blew their trumpets and shouted, **"For the LORD and for Gideon!"** Hearing hundreds of trumpet blasts and seeing hundreds of torches, the Midianites assumed that a very large army, larger than their own, had surrounded them. In the confusion, the Midianites panicked and fought among themselves.

🎭 *MIDIANITES stand and say, "There must be tens of thousands of Israelites! There's no way we can fight so many. Let's get out of here!"*

NARRATOR: Then the Midianites ran away.

🎭 *MIDIANITES remove their masks and join GIDEON and the ISRAELITES.*

NARRATOR: Gideon and his army chased the Midianites until they were no longer in the country of Israel. Gideon believed in the LORD and the LORD was with him. By faith in the LORD, Gideon was able to lead the Israelites to victory.

The Good Shepherd
Psalm 23

Casting Call:
3 Characters + Class

Masked Roles: Good Shepherd, Flock members, at least two Lions

Costumes and Props:

You will need:

Good Shepherd: mask 2 and accessories 3, 6, and 7

Flock: accessory 14 for entire class

Lions: at least two copies of accessory 13

Setting the Stage:

Keep the Lion masks in your hand for now. FLOCK stands in the middle of the room with SHEPHERD standing behind them.

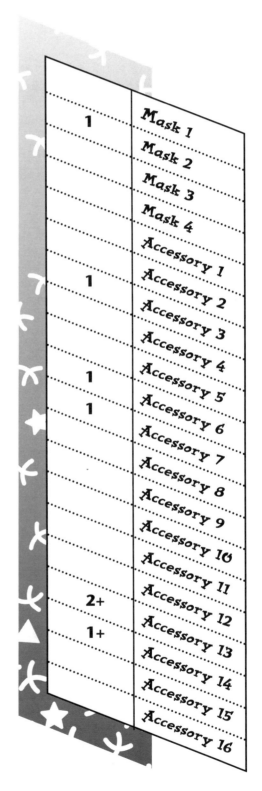

	Mask 1
1	Mask 2
	Mask 3
	Mask 4
	Accessory 1
1	Accessory 2
	Accessory 3
	Accessory 4
1	Accessory 5
1	Accessory 6
	Accessory 7
	Accessory 8
	Accessory 9
	Accessory 10
	Accessory 11
2+	Accessory 12
1+	Accessory 13
	Accessory 14
	Accessory 15
	Accessory 16

NARRATOR: The LORD is my shepherd, I shall not be in want.

FLOCK: "We are not alone—we have the Lord to take care of us."

FLOCK begins walking around room with SHEPHERD following behind.

NARRATOR: He makes me lie down in green pastures,

FLOCK: "The Lord gives us all that we need and we can rest because we know that the Lord protects us."

FLOCK lies down where they are and SHEPHERD circles them as if guarding them.

NARRATOR: He leads me beside quiet waters.

FLOCK: "When we are afraid, the Lord leads us to places where we feel safe."

FLOCK stands, then starts walking with the SHEPHERD following. FLOCK then pantomimes being afraid of something in front of them. SHEPHERD directs them to another part of the room.

NARRATOR: He restores my soul.

FLOCK: "We can have peace and happiness because the Lord sees to all our needs."

SHEPHERD walks among the FLOCK and touches each one's head. After each member of the FLOCK has been touched by the SHEPHERD, he or she acts calm.

NARRATOR: He guides me in paths of righteousness for His name's sake.

FLOCK: "Everyone who sees how happy and trusting we are of our Shepherd knows that our Lord is loving."

SHEPHERD leads the FLOCK back across the room. One SHEEP walks away from the FLOCK. The SHEPHERD goes and leads the straying SHEEP back to the FLOCK.

NARRATOR: Even though I walk through the valley of the shadow of death, I will fear no evil, for You are with me; Your rod and Your staff, they comfort me.

FLOCK: "The Lord loves us, and shows us the way to go. The Lord protects us. He will place Himself between us and our enemies and fight to defend us. We can feel safe."

Several of the FLOCK now take off their sheep masks and don the Lion masks you've been holding. The LIONS stand to one side of the FLOCK and roar. FLOCK huddles close together and follows the SHEPHERD closely as they walk past the LIONS.

NARRATOR: You prepare a table before me in the presence of my enemies.

FLOCK: "Even when we are surrounded by those who would hurt us, the Lord sees to all our needs."

SHEPHERD faces the LIONS and raises his staff. LIONS step back, but continue to roar softly. FLOCK then lies down and SHEPHERD walks around the FLOCK. LIONS stop roaring.

NARRATOR: You anoint my head with oil; my cup overflows.

FLOCK: "Because we are His, the Lord shows each one of us His loving care."

FLOCK stands up. LIONS remove their masks and put their sheep masks on again and rejoin the FLOCK. FLOCK goes to the center of the room with the SHEPHERD following.

NARRATOR: Surely goodness and love will follow me all the days of my life,

FLOCK: "We know that the Lord will show us His love and care every day of our lives."

SHEPHERD circles the standing FLOCK a couple of times.

NARRATOR: And I will dwell in the house of the Lord forever.

FLOCK: "The Lord's love and care never ends. He is with us here on earth, and someday we will be with the Lord forever in heaven."

Now lead the entire class in saying Psalm 23 in a repeat-after-me fashion.

The Lord is my shepherd, I shall not be in want.
He makes me lie down in green pastures,
He leads me beside quiet waters, He restores my soul.
He guides me in paths of righteousness for His name's sake.
Even though I walk through the valley of the shadow of death,
I will fear no evil, for You are with me; Your rod and Your staff,
they comfort me.
You prepare a table before me in the presence of my enemies.
You anoint my head with oil; my cup overflows.
Surely goodness and love will follow me all the days of my life,
and I will dwell in the house of the Lord forever.

Daniel and the Lions' Den

Daniel 6

Casting Call:
7 Characters + Class

Masked Roles: Daniel, three Friends, King Darius, two Soldiers, and Lions

Supporting Players: Court Officials, who will also portray Lions later in the skitlet

Costumes and Props:

You will need:

Daniel: mask 2 and accessory 4

Friend One: mask 2 and accessory 6

Friend Two: mask 2 and accessory 6

Friend Three: mask 2 and accessory 6

King Darius: mask 1 and accessory 15

Soldier One: mask 1 and accessories 8, 9, and 12

Soldier Two: mask 2 and accessories 8, 9, and 12

Lions: accessory 13

Setting the Stage:

DANIEL and FRIENDS stand in one corner of the room. KING and SOLDIERS stand in the center of the room. The rest of the class are COURT OFFICIALS; they stand with the KING. Keep the LION masks, one for each child portraying a COURT OFFICIAL, near at hand for use later in the skitlet.

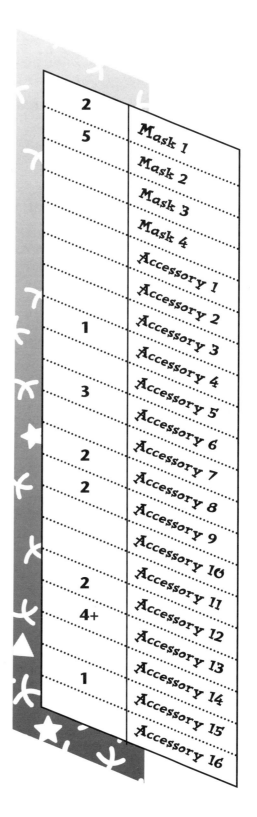

2	Mask 1
5	Mask 2
	Mask 3
	Mask 4
	Accessory 1
	Accessory 2
1	Accessory 3
	Accessory 4
3	Accessory 5
	Accessory 6
2	Accessory 7
2	Accessory 8
	Accessory 9
	Accessory 10
2	Accessory 11
4+	Accessory 12
	Accessory 13
1	Accessory 14
	Accessory 15
	Accessory 16

NARRATOR: Daniel was a young man who lived in Jerusalem. The kingdom of Babylon attacked Jerusalem. Daniel and some other young men were taken from their homes to become personal servants of the King of Babylon.

SOLDIERS walk over to DANIEL and FRIENDS and bring them to the center of the room.

NARRATOR: Although the people of Babylon worshiped many false gods, Daniel and his friends continued to worhsip the one true God, the God of Israel.

DANIEL and FRIENDS step to one side of the group, kneel, and bow their heads as though in prayer. COURT OFFICIALS say, "Those Israelites are so strange."

NARRATOR: Because of their faithfulness, God gave Daniel and his friends special gifts and talents.

DANIEL and FRIENDS stand and say, "Thank You, Lord." FRIENDS remove their masks and now portray COURT OFFICIALS.

NARRATOR: Daniel's gift was the ability to understand what dreams meant. Now it happened that the King of Babylon was having many strange and puzzling dreams.

KING says to COURT OFFICIALS, "I had a confusing dream last night ... can any of you help me understand what it means?" COURT OFFICIALS reply, "Let me tell you about a dream I had ...," and "Well, I suppose it could mean ...," and "I think it means this ..." KING turns to SOLDIERS and says, "Bring that boy Daniel to me. I've heard he can understand dreams."

NARRATOR: Daniel was brought to the king, and using the gift the Lord had given him, Daniel told the king what his dream meant. Daniel gained the king's trust and respect.

SOLDIERS bring DANIEL to the KING. KING and DANIEL step to one side of the group. KING nods his head as if agreeing with something DANIEL has said, and then says, "Daniel, you always give me such good advice. I'm going to make you one of my most trusted officials." KING and DANIEL rejoin the group and stand in the middle of it.

NARRATOR: Daniel served the kings of Babylon for many years, until finally, Daniel became a court official under King Darius. King Darius planned to make Daniel the highest court official in the land, which would give Daniel control over all the other court officials. The other court officials were jealous of Daniel, and began to think of ways they could ruin Daniel's special relationship with the king.

COURT OFFICIALS turn toward each other and say, "We can't have a foreigner telling us what to do," "We've got to do something, or we'll lose our special places serving the king," and "There must be something that Daniel does that will get him into trouble with the king."

NARRATOR: But though the court officials tried, they could find nothing that would get Daniel into trouble.

DANIEL walks away from the group and stands with head bowed. COURT OFFICIALS walk a few steps toward DANIEL, stop, and say, "That's it! Maybe we can get rid of Daniel because he still worships the God of Israel!" COURT OFFICIALS now walk back to the KING.

NARRATOR: The scheming court officials went to King Darius and said, "**We have decided you should issue a new law. For the next 30 days, anyone who prays to any other god or man but you, O king, shall be thrown into the lions' den.**"

KING says, "I like it! Let it be made the law!" DANIEL now returns to the group. SOLDIERS step forward and say, "Hear ye, hear ye! All who live in this land must worship no god but King Darius for 30 days!"

NARRATOR: Daniel heard of the new law and returned to his home to worship God.

DANIEL turns his back to the group, steps away, and kneels as if in prayer. COURT OFFICIALS go and stand behind DANIEL and say, "We've caught you breaking the law! There's no hope for you now!" COURT OFFICIALS go stand before the KING.

NARRATOR: The court officials told King Darius, "**Daniel is still worshiping his God. Because Daniel has broken your new law, he must be thrown into the lions' den.**"

COURT OFFICIALS take off their masks and put on the LION masks and stand to one side of the room.

NARRATOR: King Darius was upset. All that day he tried to think of a way to get out of having to punish Daniel, but he couldn't. He knew that once a law was made in Babylon, even the king couldn't take it back. So, very reluctantly, King Darius gave the order to have Daniel thrown into the lions' den.

SOLDIERS hold DANIEL's arms and lead him into the middle of the LIONS. KING follows behind.

NARRATOR: The king said to Daniel, "**May your God, whom you worship, rescue you!**" A stone was placed over the mouth of the lions' den, and the king returned to his palace.

SOLDIERS and KING turn away and come stand by you. Have the LIONS on their hands and knees circle the standing DANIEL, and roar and say such things as, "Mmm, dinner!" DANIEL sits down; the LIONS lie down and are quiet.

NARRATOR: King Darius was so worried about Daniel that he couldn't eat or sleep all night. The next morning, King Darius hurried to the lions' den. The king called, "**Daniel, servant of the living God, has your God been able to rescue you from the lions?**"

KING shifts from foot to foot.

NARRATOR: Then the king heard something remarkable. He heard Daniel saying, "**O king, my God sent His angel and he shut the mouths of the lions. They have not hurt me, because I did nothing that my God finds wrong. Nor have I ever done any wrong to you, O king.**" King Darius was overjoyed and said, "**Quickly! Remove Daniel out of the lions' den!**"

SOLDIERS walk DANIEL out of the circle of LIONS.

NARRATOR: After Daniel had been removed from the lions' den, he was found to be without one mark or wound from the lions. Daniel had trusted and relied on the Lord when his faith had been threatened, and he had trusted and relied on the Lord when his life was threatened. He came through both whole in body and in faith.

Jonah
The Book of Jonah

Casting Call:
4 Characters + Class

Masked Roles: Jonah, Captain/Ninevite, and Sailors/Ninevites

Supporting Roles: Vine, Worm

Costumes and Props:

You will need:

Jonah: mask 1 and accessory 6

Captain: mask 2 and accessories 4, 5, and 6

Sailors: masks 1 and 2 and accessories 3, 4, 5, and 6—you will remove accessory 5 from Captain and Sailors masks when they portray the Ninevites

Setting the Stage:

CAPTAIN and SAILORS stand in center of room and form a boat shape. JONAH stands next to you.

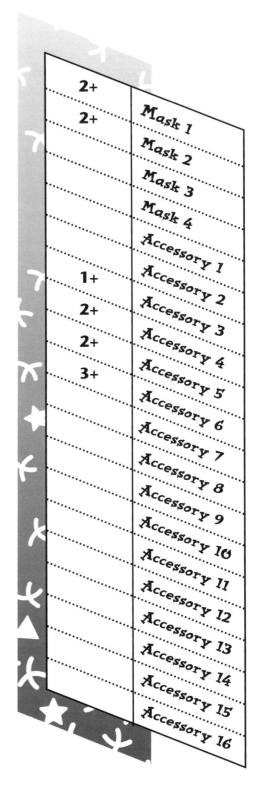

2+	
2+	Mask 1
	Mask 2
	Mask 3
	Mask 4
	Accessory 1
1+	Accessory 2
2+	Accessory 3
2+	Accessory 4
3+	Accessory 5
	Accessory 6
	Accessory 7
	Accessory 8
	Accessory 9
	Accessory 10
	Accessory 11
	Accessory 12
	Accessory 13
	Accessory 14
	Accessory 15
	Accessory 16

NARRATOR: Jonah was a prophet of the LORD. That means God used Jonah to tell others about His purpose and plans. Sometimes this meant Jonah had to tell people things they didn't want to hear, and sometimes this meant Jonah had to do things he didn't want to do. One time, instead of going to Nineveh as God had told him to, Jonah decided to run away from the LORD. Jonah went to the port city of Joppa.

🎭 JONAH walks to where CAPTAIN and SAILORS are and says, **"Where is your ship heading?"** CAPTAIN answers, **"Tarshish."** JONAH says, **"Good, that's about as far away from Nineveh as you can get, and that's exactly what I want."**

NARRATOR: Jonah boarded the ship and went down below to sleep.

🎭 JONAH lies down in the middle of the boat shape formed by SAILORS and CAPTAIN. SAILORS and CAPTAIN bend their knees and rise up and down.

NARRATOR: The LORD sent a great storm, and the ship was in danger of sinking. The sailors on the ship were very afraid.

🎭 SAILORS say, **"Captain! What can we do? We're going to sink!"** CAPTAIN says, **"Throw some of the cargo into the sea; maybe that will help us stay afloat."**

NARRATOR: As the sailors began to throw cargo overboard, they each began to call out prayers to their gods for help and comfort. The captain went to get Jonah. The captain found Jonah asleep and woke him up.

🎭 CAPTAIN kneels beside JONAH and gently shakes JONAH's shoulder.

NARRATOR: The captain said, **"How can you sleep? Get up and call on your god! Maybe he will take notice of us, and we will not perish."**

🎭 CAPTAIN and JONAH stand up.

NARRATOR: Jonah went up to the deck. The sailors decided to find out who was to blame for this catastrophe.

🎭 CAPTAIN, JONAH, and SAILORS turn toward each other and do "Rock, Paper, Scissors" motions.

NARRATOR: The sailors said, **"It's you, Jonah. Where are you from and what did you do to cause this?"** Jonah told them, **"I am a Hebrew, and I worship the LORD, the God of heaven, who made the sea and land."** The sailors asked, **"What did you do to make your god so angry with you?"** Jonah answered, **"My LORD, God of Israel, told me to go to Nineveh and tell the people of that city that they will be destroyed for all the wrong things they do. I'm trying to run away from God, but now I know that I can't."** The sailors then asked, **"What can we do to make this storm stop?"** Jonah replied, **"Since it's my fault that this storm is putting all of you at risk, pick me up and throw me in the sea, and it will become calm."** But the sailors couldn't bring themselves to throw Jonah overboard. The sea was so rough they knew he would drown.

🎭 CAPTAIN and SAILORS sit on either side of JONAH, who remains standing, and pantomime rowing. CAPTAIN chants, **"Heave! Ho! Heave! Ho!"**

NARRATOR: So the sailors tried to row the boat to shore. But the sea became even wilder.

🎭 *CAPTAIN and two SAILORS gather around JONAH. SAILORS each hold one of JONAH's arms.*

NARRATOR: The sailors finally gathered around Jonah and said, "**Oh, LORD, please do not let us die for taking this man's life. Do not hold us accountable for killing an innocent man, for now we know that You, O LORD, are in control.**" Then they took Jonah and threw him overboard, and the sea grew calm.

🎭 *SAILORS holding JONAH's arms walk him outside of the boat shape. SAILORS and CAPTAIN wait for your signal to regroup as a whale.*

NARRATOR: Jonah prayed to the LORD as he began sinking in the water.

🎭 *JONAH kneels, bows his head, and folds his hands in prayer.*

NARRATOR: The LORD heard Jonah's prayer, and had Jonah swallowed by a big fish.

🎭 *SAILORS and CAPTAIN now come and surround JONAH in the shape of a whale, leaving an opening at one end. JONAH remains kneeling.*

NARRATOR: Jonah was in the belly of the fish for three days and three nights. Jonah prayed to the LORD. Jonah prayed, "**Thank You, LORD, for hearing my prayer. Thank You, LORD, for saving me from the sea. Because I am thankful, I will do as You have asked me. Salvation comes from You.**" The LORD then had the fish spit up Jonah onto dry land.

🎭 *JONAH crawls through the opening left by the SAILORS and CAPTAIN in their portrayal of the whale. Then SAILORS and CAPTAIN remove their accessory 5 attachments, and gather on one side of the room to become the NINEVITES.*

NARRATOR: The LORD told Jonah for the second time, "Go to the great city of Nineveh and tell all who live there the message I have given you." Jonah obeyed this time, and went to Nineveh.

🎭 *JONAH goes to the NINEVITES and walks around the group three times.*

NARRATOR: It took three days for Jonah to walk through the great city of Nineveh. As he did, Jonah called out, "**Forty more days and Nineveh will be destroyed.**"

🎭 *Once JONAH has circled the NINEVITES three times, have him continue to say softly, "**Forty more days and Nineveh will be destroyed.**"*

NARRATOR: The Ninevites believed what the LORD was saying through his prophet Jonah. The Ninevites were very sorry they had offended God and turned away from their sinful ways.

🎭 *NINEVITES react and say, "**The LORD God of Israel is angry with us. We must change our ways and live as God wants us to.**"*

NARRATOR: The Ninevites went without food or drink to show God how sorry they were. God saw that the Ninevites truly meant to change their ways and were sorry for having angered Him. God took pity on them, and through His mercy, decided not to destroy Nineveh after all.

🎭 *NINEVITES say, "**Praise the LORD God of Israel! He has shown us mercy!**" JONAH stands back from the NINEVITES with arms crossed, looking angry.*

NARRATOR: Jonah became angry at the LORD. He said, "LORD, I knew You would have pity on the Ninevites! I knew You would not destroy their city! That's why I tried to run away from You. I knew because You are so loving and kind, if the Ninevites changed their ways, You would let them live! Now LORD, **let me die, for it would be better than to go on living!**"

JONAH stomps off six or seven feet from the NINEVITES, and sits down.

NARRATOR: Jonah went off and built a shelter outside the great city of Nineveh and waited and watched. Jonah was probably still hoping God would destroy the Ninevites. Jonah, who had so recently thanked God for His mercy in letting him live, now wanted to die rather than see the God of Israel have mercy on people who were not Israelites. Jonah was very mad at God.

The child portraying the VINE separates from the NINEVITE group and crouches down near JONAH.

NARRATOR: Jonah didn't have much shade from the hot sun, so God caused a vine to grow that protected Jonah from the sun.

VINE slowly rises up and stands over JONAH with hands outstretched over JONAH's head.

NARRATOR: Jonah was very happy that God provided shade for him. He felt that it was proof of his very special relationship with the LORD.

The child portraying the WORM separates from NINEVITES and crawls to the feet of VINE.

NARRATOR: But at dawn the next day, God sent a worm that chewed the vine, which made it wither and die.

VINE sinks slowly to the ground. VINE and WORM return to NINEVITES.

NARRATOR: When the sun rose, God sent a scorching hot wind and the sun blazed on Jonah's head. Jonah was miserable. Again he told the LORD, **"It would be better if I died!"** The LORD asked, "Do you have a right to be angry?" Jonah said, **"Yes, I do! I am angry enough to die!"** But the LORD said, "You were happy with Me when I provided a vine to give you comfort." Jonah replied, **"Yes, but then You took it away from me."** The LORD said, "I caused it to grow and then I caused it to die. It was part of My creation. Its life and death had nothing to do with you."

JONAH crosses arms and says, "You could have at least let it live long enough for me to have shade! You certainly don't do things the way I would do them!"

NARRATOR: The LORD said, "You are not really angry with Me about the vine. You are angry with Me because I had mercy on Nineveh. Should I not be as concerned about those people as I am with you?"

Have JONAH get up and walk off to the side of the room.

NARRATOR: No one knows how long Jonah stayed mad at God. Perhaps Jonah eventually came to understand the grace and mercy of God. For God takes no pleasure in the death of people who sin against Him, or don't believe in Him. Rather, He wants everyone to change their ways and believe in Him.

Miraculous Faith

Matthew 8:5–13; Luke 8:40–56

Casting Call:
6 Characters + Class

Masked Roles: Jesus, at least one Disciple, Centurion, Sick Woman, Jairus, and Jairus' Daughter

Supporting Roles: Jairus' Servant, Jairus' Wife, Mourners

Costumes and Props:

You will need:

Jesus: mask 2 and accessory 3

Disciples: mask 2 and accessory 4

Centurion: mask 1 and accessories 8, 9, and 12

Sick Woman: mask 3 and accessory 2

Jairus: mask 1 and accessories 4 and 6

Jairus' Daughter: mask 4 and accessory 1

Setting the Stage:

JESUS stands in the center of the room, with CROWD standing around him. All the other characters are within the crowd. DISCIPLES stand closest to JESUS.

Count	Item
2	
1+	Mask 1
1	Mask 2
1	Mask 3
1	Mask 4
1	Accessory 1
1	Accessory 2
2+	Accessory 3
	Accessory 4
1	Accessory 5
	Accessory 6
	Accessory 7
1	Accessory 8
1	Accessory 9
	Accessory 10
	Accessory 11
1	Accessory 12
	Accessory 13
	Accessory 14
	Accessory 15
	Accessory 16

NARRATOR: Jesus was teaching one day and a large crowd was gathered all around Him.

CROWD says things like, "But Jesus, how can You compare faith with a mustard seed?" and "How can I believe in what I can't see or touch?"

NARRATOR: The crowd was pushing so close to Jesus they were almost crushing Him.

DISCIPLES stand with arms outstretched and say, "Please don't push, the Teacher has time for all of you."

NARRATOR: A Roman soldier made his way to stand before Jesus. He was no ordinary soldier; he was a centurion, which meant he had 100 soldiers in his care.

CENTURION makes his way through CROWD to stand before JESUS.

NARRATOR: The centurion said to Jesus, **"Lord, I need Your help. My servant is very sick and he is in a lot of pain."** Jesus replied, **"I will go and heal him."** The centurion replied, **"Oh, no Lord. I don't deserve to have you actually come to my house. Besides, that's not even necessary."**

CROWD says, "What can he mean? Of course Jesus must go in person to heal the sick servant."

NARRATOR: The centurion told Jesus, **"All You have to do, Lord, is say the word, and my servant will be healed."**

CROWD asks, "How can that be?"

NARRATOR: The centurion said, **"I understand a little bit about authority and the power that goes with it. I have been given the authority to say to people, "Go," and they go; and that one, "Come," and he comes. I say to one of my servants, "Do this," and he does it. You have the authority to say, "Be healed," and it will be done just as You say."** When Jesus heard this, He was amazed. Turning to the crowd following Him, He said, **"I tell you, I have not found such great faith even in Israel."** Jesus had been rejected as the Son of God by many of His own people, yet here was a Roman soldier who had great faith and trust in Jesus' authority from God. So Jesus said to the centurion, **"Go! It will be done just as you believed it would."** And the centurion's servant was healed at that very hour.

CENTURION leaves the circle of the CROWD, removes mask and accessories, and rejoins the class as one of the CROWD. JAIRUS and JAIRUS' DAUGHTER step from the CROWD and move across the room. The DAUGHTER lies down, and JAIRUS kneels beside her. JESUS, DISCIPLES, and CROWD walk around the room once, and CROWD pushes close to JESUS and DISCIPLES. DISCIPLES say, "I tell you, Jesus has time for all of you. Give Him room!"

NARRATOR: Another day, Jesus was teaching once again and surrounded by a large crowd. A man name Jairus made his way through the crowd to Jesus.

🎭 *JAIRUS approaches CROWD and makes his way to kneel before JESUS.*

NARRATOR: Jairus fell at Jesus' feet and said, **"O Lord, my little girl is sick! We're afraid she will die. Please come and heal her."**

🎭 *CROWD says, "But Jesus, I need You too!" "Listen to me!" and "Jesus, what should I do about my problem?" JESUS, JAIRUS, DISCIPLES, and CROWD then move halfway to where JAIRUS' DAUGHTER is lying down.*

NARRATOR: Jesus went with Jairus to his house, with the crowd still pushing close to Jesus to try to get His attention. A woman was in the crowd who had been sick for many years. None of the doctors she had seen had been able to heal her. Seeing Jesus, she thought, **"If I can just touch His robe, I know that I will be healed."**

🎭 *SICK WOMAN, who has been part of the CROWD, tiptoes to stand next to JESUS.*

NARRATOR: So the woman made her way to Jesus, and without anyone noticing, she touched the edge of Jesus' robe. Immediately, she was healed of her illness.

🎭 *SICK WOMAN moves to outer edge of CROWD and kneels down as if in prayer.*

NARRATOR: Jesus asked, **"Who touched Me?"** All the people near Jesus denied touching Him.

🎭 *Everyone in CROWD takes a step back and says, "Not me!" "Not me, Teacher!" JESUS looks around as if searching for a specific person.*

NARRATOR: His disciples asked Jesus, **"With all these people crowding around and pushing against You, how can You ask who touched You?"** But that isn't what Jesus meant. Jesus didn't mean the touching that happens in a large crowd with people pushing and bumping each other. Jesus knew that someone had touched Him to be healed. Jesus said, **"I know that someone touched Me."** Jesus wouldn't move until He found out who had been healed by touching Him.

🎭 *SICK WOMAN stands and walks reluctantly back to JESUS, afraid that she's in trouble. She kneels at JESUS' feet.*

NARRATOR: Finally, the woman made her way back through the crowd to Jesus. She was afraid she would get in trouble for bothering Him. She knelt at Jesus' feet, and said, **"O Lord, I didn't mean to bother You. But I knew that if I could just touch even Your robe, You could heal me of this illness. And it is true—touching You healed me."** Then Jesus told her, **"Daughter, your faith has healed you. Go in peace."** The woman had come to Jesus for help, but had been too afraid to ask Him. By insisting that she come forward, Jesus was able to make sure she would never feel bad about what she had done.

🎭 *SICK WOMAN removes mask and rejoins CROWD. A member of CROWD becomes JAIRUS' SERVANT.*

NARRATOR: A servant of Jairus' came to Jairus and said, **"Don't bother the Teacher anymore, your daughter is dead."**

JAIRUS hangs his head. JESUS puts his hand upon JAIRUS' back and says, "Don't be afraid; just believe, and she will be healed." JAIRUS nods his head, and then leads JESUS, DISCIPLES, and CROWD to where JAIRUS' DAUGHTER is lying down. As they move, CROWD says, "But it's too late! She is beyond help now."

NARRATOR: Jairus led Jesus to his house, and the crowd followed them there. People outside Jairus' house were already crying from grief.

Several of CROWD become MOURNERS and say loudly, "Oh, she is gone!" and "Oh, poor Jairus!"

NARRATOR: Jesus told the mourners, **"Stop crying. She is not dead but asleep."** The mourners laughed at Him, and said, **"We have seen her dead body with our own eyes."**

One of CROWD becomes JAIRUS' WIFE and says to JAIRUS, "Oh you are too late! There is no hope now." JAIRUS replies, "I will believe what Jesus said even though I don't see how He can help anymore." JESUS, JAIRUS, and DISCIPLES kneel down by JAIRUS' DAUGHTER. CROWD and MOURNERS step back.

NARRATOR: Jesus would not let anyone in Jairus' house but Himself, Jairus, and the disciples.

JESUS holds JAIRUS' DAUGHTER's hand.

NARRATOR: Jesus took the girl by the hand and said, **"My child, get up!"** At once, the girl stood up.

JAIRUS' DAUGHTER stands. CROWD cheers.

NARRATOR: All three people who asked Jesus for healing that day had their faith rewarded. The centurion came to Jesus with complete trust in Jesus' ability to heal the sick. The sick woman came fearfully to Jesus, not fully trusting Jesus would think she was worth healing. She had hoped she could go unnoticed by Jesus, but Jesus took the time to tell her Himself that she was healed. Jairus kept his faith in Jesus' ability to heal his daughter, even though he did need some encouragement from the Lord when things looked bad.

We all experience these different types of faith, sometimes even on the same day! Let the love and concern Jesus showed for these three believers help you understand the love and concern Jesus shows to you every day.

Feeding of the 5,000

Matthew 14:13–21; Luke 9:10–15; and John 6:1–13

Casting Call:
13 Characters + Class

Masked Roles: Jesus, up to 12 Disciples

Supporting Players: Young Boy, Crowd

Costumes and Props:

You will need:

Jesus: mask 2 and accessory 3

Disciples: masks 1 and 2 and accessories 3, 4, 5, and 6

Basket: one for each child in class

Fish: one for each child in class

Bread: one for each child in class

Setting the Stage:

JESUS stands on one side of the room and CROWD gathers around him. DISCIPLES stand near you with their baskets in hand. Give one of the CROWD members a basket containing a fish cutout and a loaf cutout for each child in class. This child will portray the YOUNG BOY later in the skitlet.

6	
7	Mask 1
	Mask 2
	Mask 3
	Mask 4
	Accessory 1
13	Accessory 2
12	Accessory 3
12	Accessory 4
12	Accessory 5
	Accessory 6
	Accessory 7
	Accessory 8
	Accessory 9
	Accessory 10
	Accessory 11
	Accessory 12
	Accessory 13
	Accessory 14
	Accessory 15
	Accessory 16

NARRATOR: Jesus was teaching one day in a small town near a lake. He was telling people about God.

DISCIPLES go and stand next to JESUS in the middle of the CROWD.

NARRATOR: While Jesus was teaching, His disciples came to tell Him some sad news.

*DISCIPLES say, "**John the Baptist, the one whom God sent to tell the world about You, has been killed.**" JESUS bows his head for a moment. CROWD says, "**Jesus, please tell us more about our Father,**" and "**I need to talk to You!**" and "**Listen to me, Jesus! Listen to me!**"*

NARRATOR: The disciples tried to tell Jesus everything else they had done while they had been away from Him, but the crowd was so large and noisy they couldn't. Jesus said to His disciples, "**Come with Me to a quiet place and get some rest.**" So Jesus and His disciples got into a boat to cross the lake so they could be alone to talk, eat, and rest.

*JESUS and DISCIPLES stand in front of CROWD, facing away from them. CROWD says, "**Jesus, don't go! I want to learn more!**" and "**Let's follow Jesus!**"*

NARRATOR: But the crowd saw them leaving and ran along the shoreline of the lake. The crowd reached the other side of the lake before Jesus and the disciples did.

JESUS and DISCIPLES begin to slowly walk across the room. CROWD quickly walks along one side of the room and stands on the other side, facing JESUS and DISCIPLES.

NARRATOR: When Jesus and the disciples' boat reached the shore, Jesus saw the large crowds and He had compassion for them.

*CROWD surrounds JESUS once again, leaving the DISCIPLES standing on one side. CROWD says, "**Please, Teacher, You have to help me!**" and "**Please, Jesus, heal me,**" and "**What does 'kingdom of God' mean?**"*

NARRATOR: So Jesus spoke to the large crowd about the kingdom of God and healed those who needed healing.

DISCIPLES come stand next to JESUS in the middle of the CROWD.

NARRATOR: As evening approached, the disciples came to Him and said, "**This is a remote place, and it's already very late. Send the people away so they can go buy themselves something to eat.**" But Jesus answered, "**They do not need to go away. You give them something to eat.**" One disciple said, "**But eight months' wages wouldn't buy enough bread for each one in this crowd to have one bite!**" There were at least 5,000 men gathered around Jesus and His disciples, plus all the women and children.

One DISCIPLE turns to the YOUNG BOY and takes his basket from him.

NARRATOR: One of the disciples said, **"Here is a boy with five small barley loaves and two small fish, but how far will they go among so many?"** Jesus said, **"Bring them to Me."** Jesus then told all the people to sit down on the grass.

CROWD spreads out a little, then sits down.

NARRATOR: Jesus took the five loaves and two fish and, looking up to heaven, He gave thanks and broke the loaves. He did the same with the fish.

JESUS holds up one of the loaf cutouts and one of the fish cutouts and says, "Father, I give You thanks for this food that You have provided." JESUS then opens the cutouts so that two pictures of each show.

NARRATOR: Then He gave them to His disciples to set before the people.

JESUS hands each DISCIPLE a loaf and a fish cutout and DISCIPLES give them to each person in the CROWD.

NARRATOR: All the people ate as much as they wanted.

CROWD places their loaf and fish cutouts on the floor in front of them.

NARRATOR: Then Jesus told the disciples, **"Gather the pieces that are left over. Let nothing be wasted."**

DISCIPLES pick up the cutouts on the floor and put them into their baskets.

NARRATOR: So the disciples picked up the leftovers from those five little loaves and two small fish … and all twelve of their baskets were full. God didn't just provide enough to eat for that one meal, He gave so much that the disciples had enough to eat for a week. Just as God miraculously fed all those people hungry for food, Jesus' teachings fed all those who were hungry for the Word of God.

Fishers of Men

Luke 5:1–11

Casting Call:
5 Characters + Class

Masked Roles: Jesus, Simon Peter, Andrew, James, and John.

Supporting Players: Crowd

Costumes and Props:

You will need:

Jesus: mask 2 and accessory 3

Simon Peter: mask 2 and accessories 4 and 5

Andrew: mask 2 and accessories 5 and 6

James: mask 2 and accessories 4 and 6

John: mask 2 and accessory 5

Setting the Stage:

JESUS stands in the center of the room. SIMON PETER and ANDREW sit cross-legged facing each other behind JESUS. JAMES and JOHN sit cross-legged several feet to one side of SIMON PETER and ANDREW. The rest of the class should remain by your side. They will become the CROWD.

5	Mask 1
	Mask 2
	Mask 3
	Mask 4
	Accessory 1
1	Accessory 2
2	Accessory 3
3	Accessory 4
2	Accessory 5
	Accessory 6
	Accessory 7
	Accessory 8
	Accessory 9
	Accessory 10
	Accessory 11
	Accessory 12
	Accessory 13
	Accessory 14
	Accessory 15
	Accessory 16

NARRATOR: When Jesus first began His teaching, He was all alone.

JESUS says, "I bring you good news! The kingdom of God is near!" Send several of the children near you to surround JESUS and say, "Tell us more!"

NARRATOR: Soon Jesus had many people who would come listen to His teachings, so many that Jesus needed help.

Send remaining children near you to surround JESUS. CROWD says, "Jesus, tell us more!" and "Tell the parable about the sower again!"

NARRATOR: One day, Jesus was teaching on the shore of the Sea of Galilee. There were so many people eager to hear His teachings that Jesus was in danger of being pushed into the water.

JESUS takes several steps backward to stand just in front of SIMON PETER and ANDREW.

NARRATOR: Nearby, two fishermen named Simon Peter and Andrew were sitting in their fishing boat cleaning their nets.

SIMON PETER says to ANDREW, "I'm so tired." ANDREW says, "Me too. I can't believe we fished all night and didn't catch a thing." JESUS turns to face SIMON PETER and ANDREW.

NARRATOR: Jesus saw Simon Peter and Andrew. He asked them if He could get in their boat and finish teaching from there.

SIMON PETER and ANDREW stand up. JESUS stands between SIMON PETER and ANDREW and faces CROWD.

NARRATOR: From the boat, a little distance from the shore, Jesus was able to continue His teaching. When He was finished, Jesus said to Simon Peter, **"Put out into deep water, and let down the nets for a catch."** Simon Peter said, **"We've worked hard all night and haven't caught anything. But because You say so, I will let down the fishing nets again."**

SIMON PETER turns to one side and makes a two-handed throwing motion. ANDREW stands by SIMON PETER's side. ANDREW says, "Do you really think we're going to catch any fish now?" SIMON PETER says, "I don't know. But Jesus told me to do it." CROWD then circles around and stands in front of where SIMON PETER has made his casting motion. SIMON PETER and ANDREW make hauling motions and CROWD walks slowly toward SIMON PETER, ANDREW, and JESUS.

NARRATOR: Simon Peter and Andrew began to pull the net back into their boat. To their surprise, the net was now so full of fish they couldn't pull it into their boat.

SIMON PETER and ANDREW stop hauling motions, and the CROWD stops moving. SIMON PETER and ANDREW call to JAMES and JOHN, "Come help us! We can't do this alone!" JAMES and JOHN get up and come make hauling motions along with SIMON PETER and ANDREW. The CROWD continues to move toward them, then stops on the other side of them.

NARRATOR: Simon Peter, Andrew, James, and John all worked together to pull the net in. There were so many fish that both boats were full and there were still more fish in the net.

Have all DISCIPLES say, "I can't believe this! We've caught more fish than we usually do in a week!"

NARRATOR: Jesus had repaid the fishermen's kindness to Him with such an abundance of fish that the fishermen were all amazed.

CROWD now spreads out around the room in groups of two or three. SIMON PETER kneels before JESUS.

NARRATOR: Simon Peter knelt at Jesus' feet and said, **"Go away from me, Lord, for I am a sinner. I am not worthy of Your company, nor of Your kindness."** Being in the presence of the Son of God made Simon Peter remember all the wrong things he had done in his life, and he didn't feel that he deserved Jesus' kindness. But Jesus knew Simon Peter's heart. While Simon Peter might have done wrong things in his life, Jesus knew that Simon Peter would love Him, the Lord, with all his heart.

JESUS places His hand upon the head of the still kneeling SIMON PETER.

NARRATOR: Jesus said to Simon Peter, **"Don't be afraid. Come, follow Me, and I will make you a fisher of men."** So Simon Peter became one of the first of Jesus' closest followers, called disciples, and helped Him in His work.

ANDREW, JAMES, and JOHN come and kneel at JESUS' feet.

NARRATOR: Jesus said to Andrew, James, and John, **"Follow Me."** Andrew, James, and John left everything and became His followers too.

JESUS, SIMON PETER, ANDREW, JAMES, and JOHN now walk together to each group of class members spread throughout the room. Then JESUS comes and stands by you.

NARRATOR: Simon Peter and the rest of the disciples truly became fishers of men as they followed Jesus. They were able to tell many people about the love of God and His Son, Jesus. Even after Jesus' death and resurrection, the disciples continued to "fish" for men by spreading the Gospel.

A Father's Love

Luke 15:11–32

Casting Call:
4 Characters + Class

Masked Roles: Father, Older Son, Younger Son, and Chorus

Supporting Players: Chorus; Chorus members will also be the Servant and Friends of Younger Son

Costumes and Props:

You will need:

Father: mask 1 and accessory 3

Older Son: mask 2 and accessory 4 and 6

Younger Son: mask 2 and accessory 4

Chorus: assortment of masks and accessories; just make sure that the Father, Older and Younger Son are distinct in some way.

Setting the Stage:

Prepare CHORUS by telling them they will mimic some of the words and actions of the three main characters. Develop a signal that the CHORUS will respond to by moving to stand by the character in focus. OLDER SON and YOUNGER SON stand on one side of the room. FATHER and CHORUS stand in the center of the room.

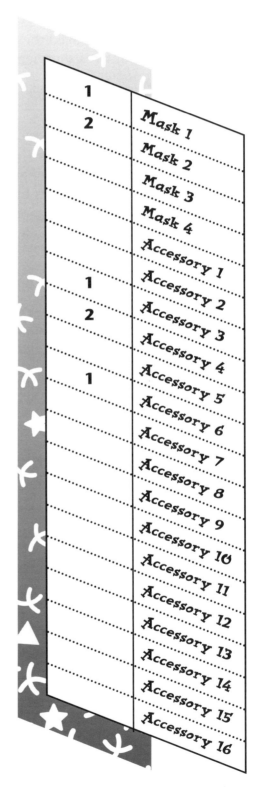

1	
2	Mask 1
	Mask 2
	Mask 3
	Mask 4
	Accessory 1
1	Accessory 2
2	Accessory 3
	Accessory 4
1	Accessory 5
	Accessory 6
	Accessory 7
	Accessory 8
	Accessory 9
	Accessory 10
	Accessory 11
	Accessory 12
	Accessory 13
	Accessory 14
	Accessory 15
	Accessory 16

NARRATOR: I am the owner of a great deal of property. There is a lot of work involved in caring for so much property. However, I have two sons to help me with my work.

FATHER and CHORUS walk over to the two SONS. CHORUS shifts to stand by the two SONS. CHORUS and SONS do hoeing motions. CHORUS will echo the SONS' lines.

NARRATOR: My older son does all that I ask of him without complaining. When I tell him, "**After you finish hoeing this field, bring in the cattle,**" my older son says, "**Yes, Father.**" My younger son, however, is very different. When I tell my younger son, "**After you finish hoeing this field, go see that the sheep have water.**" My younger son asks, "**Why? Can't one of the servants do it?**" It used to be that after I explained why I needed him to do it, he would. But now he says things like "**Why should I?**" or "**I don't feel like doing that right now.**" I tell him, "**We have so much to take care of that I need your help to get it all done,**" but my younger son doesn't listen, or maybe he just doesn't understand.

YOUNGER SON and CHORUS stop work motions and stand with their arms crossed facing the FATHER.

NARRATOR: One day, my younger son said, "**I just wish you would leave me alone and let me do the things I want to do, the way I want to do them.**"

CHORUS shifts to the FATHER.

NARRATOR: I tried to explain to my younger son, "**I am teaching you my way of doing things because I know that they are best.**"

CHORUS shifts behind YOUNGER SON.

NARRATOR: My younger son replied, "**Well, I want my share of the property right now, so that I can leave here, leave you, and find my own way in the world.**"

CHORUS shifts to the FATHER.

NARRATOR: I reluctantly agreed. I divided all my property and belongings in half. I sold the portion that would have been my younger son's inheritance and gave the money to him. He took the money, and set out on his trip.

YOUNGER SON turns his back on FATHER and walks to the other side of the room. CHORUS gathers by OLDER SON.

NARRATOR: I was very sad to see my younger son leave me, but it was his decision, and I had to let my younger son go. My older son said, "**Good riddance! You can count on me to see that everything is done right.**"

CHORUS gathers by FATHER.

NARRATOR: I nodded to my older son and said, "**Yes, Son, I can always count on you to stay with me. But I pray your brother returns to us some day.**"

FATHER and OLDER SON come stand next to you. CHORUS joins YOUNGER SON on other side of the room.

NARRATOR: I was so happy when I left my father. I felt so free. Anything I wanted to do, I could.

YOUNGER SON and CHORUS say, "I'm free! No one can tell me what to do!"

NARRATOR: With money in my pocket, I quickly found all kinds of fun things to do. At one point, I noticed that most of my money was gone, but I still had enough to keep having fun with my friends.

CHORUS members surrounding YOUNGER SON leave the group one by one and come stand by you.

NARRATOR: Eventually, all my money was gone, and so were my friends.

YOUNGER SON stands in the center of the room. CHORUS rejoins the YOUNGER SON. FATHER and OLDER SON continue to stand next to you.

NARRATOR: I was beginning to think, **"Maybe my father was right."** But I was determined to make my own way. I wasn't going to go back to my father, *no way*. He would just remind me of all the things I had done wrong. I couldn't face him. So I decided to find a job.

YOUNGER SON and CHORUS begin making working motions.

NARRATOR: The only job I could find was feeding pigs, dirty and smelly work. I worked all day every day and was so tired I couldn't think more than a day ahead. The pigs I fed were eating better than I was. I remembered the food my father's servants ate. Even those servants had more than I did. My father's rules and demands had seemed so hard and unfair at the time, but it would be a pleasure to work for him compared to my current job. I had been disobedient and ungrateful, but perhaps if I go back he will let me stay. I will go to him and say, **"Oh, Father, I am so sorry! I have sinned aginst you by not obeying you."** Maybe then he'll at least let me work as his servant.

YOUNGER SON and CHORUS slowly walk around the perimeter of the room while the FATHER goes to the center of the room. OLDER SON remains standing by you. Once the YOUNGER SON and CHORUS are opposite the FATHER, have them stop. CHORUS moves to stand by the FATHER and says the SERVANT's lines.

NARRATOR: One day a servant called to me, **"Sir, there is a man coming. He looks filthy and dirty. Should I get the guards and tell him to go away?"** I shaded my eyes and looked in the direction my servant was pointing. I said, **"No, the guards won't be necessary. It just looks like a traveler who has lost his way."** But as the figure got closer, I thought, **"Could it be?"** My heart began pounding and I couldn't breathe. **"Could it really be my younger son? This dirty, ragged, and worn out traveler is what is left of my proud and stubborn son?"** It was! I started running toward him.

FATHER and CHORUS walk toward the YOUNGER SON and surround him, then walk back with him to the center of the room. CHORUS now stands by the YOUNGER SON.

NARRATOR: How happy I was to see him! I gave him a hug, but he pulled back from me and, with his head down, said, **"Father, I have sinned against heaven and against you. I am no longer worthy to be called your son."** I turned to the servant and said, **"Quick! Bring the best robe and put it on him. Put a ring on his finger and sandals on his feet. Prepare the fattened calf and let's have a feast to celebrate! My son, my beloved son, who we thought was dead, is alive! My son, my beloved son, who had lost his way, is found!"** We began to celebrate.

OLDER SON now goes and stands to one side of the group in the center of the room. CHORUS shifts to stand beside him and repeats the SERVANT's lines.

NARRATOR: My oldest son, who was out working in the field, heard the music and came to the house. He asked a servant, **"What's going on?"** The servant told him, **"Your brother has returned safe and sound, so your father is throwing a party for him."** When he heard this, the older son became angry and refused to go into the party.

OLDER SON and CHORUS turn their backs to the FATHER and the YOUNGER SON and cross their arms. FATHER approaches OLDER SON. CHORUS repeats the lines of the OLDER SON.

NARRATOR: I went to my older son and said, **"Please come in and help celebrate the return of your brother."** He refused and said, **"All these years I've been slaving away for you and never disobeyed your rules, yet you've never thrown a party for me. But when this son of yours—I will not call him my brother after the way he's treated us—when he returns from wasting your money, you throw a party for him. Well, I will not celebrate his return."** I said, **"My son, you are always with me, and everything I have is yours. It is only right that we celebrate and be happy, because this brother of yours was dead to us and now is here to live with us again; he was lost and now is found."**

FATHER and CHORUS rejoin the YOUNGER SON. OLDER SON remains standing apart.

NARRATOR: Did the older son stay angry with his father and refuse to welcome his brother back home? Or did he come to understand his father's love for his brother? We don't know what the older son did. We hope he finally forgave his brother and leaned to love him. If so, there really would have been a cause for celebration.

The Full Armor of God

Ephesians 6:10–18 and 2 Chronicles 20:1–28

Casting Call:

2 Characters + Class

Masked Roles: Jehoshaphat and Judaites; one of the Judaites will play Jahaziel.

Costumes and Props:

You will need:

Jehoshaphat and Judaites: masks 1, 2, 3, 4, and accessories 1, 2, 3, 4, 8, 9, 10, 11, and 12

Setting the Stage:

Keep two JUDAITES next to you. Since all children will be wearing soldier accessories for this skitlet, choose one child to portray JEHOSHAPHAT. JEHOSHAPHAT stands in the center of the room. The rest of the JUDAITES scatter around the room.

1+	
1+	Mask 1
1+	Mask 2
1+	Mask 3
1+	Mask 4
1+	Accessory 1
1+	Accessory 2
1+	Accessory 3
	Accessory 4
	Accessory 5
	Accessory 6
1+	Accessory 7
1+	Accessory 8
1+	Accessory 9
1+	Accessory 10
1+	Accessory 11
	Accessory 12
	Accessory 13
	Accessory 14
	Accessory 15
	Accessory 16

NARRATOR: Look at what you are wearing—it is armor like soldiers wore long ago. Armor helped protect the soldiers from their enemies' weapons. Usually, no soldier would have gone into battle without his armor, but we're going to hear the story of a king and his people who did. They went into battle without wearing any armor for protection.

The two JUDAITES next to you go and stand next to JEHOSHAPHAT.

NARRATOR: Long ago, there was a king named Jehoshaphat. One day, some of his men came and told him, **"A huge army is coming to attack us."**

JEHOSHAPHAT says, "I know what we need to do!" Two JUDAITES say, "You've already figured out how we can fight our enemies? What's your plan?"

NARRATOR: Jehoshaphat's plan was to ask the LORD what to do. Jehoshaphat said, **"We must all pray for the LORD's help. This prayer is so important that I want everyone to go without food for one day to prepare themselves."**

JUDAITES scattered around room now come and gather around JEHOSHAPHAT and the two JUDAITES.

NARRATOR: The Judaite people listened to their king. They all fasted for one day. Then they came from every town in Judah to join Jehoshaphat in prayer to the LORD.

JEHOSHAPHAT and JUDAITES all remove their face masks with the helmet accessories. JUDAITES all kneel with heads bowed. JEHOSHAPHAT remains standing.

NARRATOR: Jehoshaphat stood up in front of all the Judaites and prayed for God's help. Jehoshaphat said, **"We do not know what to do, but we will do as You want us to, LORD."**

One of the kneeling JUDAITES stands up.

NARRATOR: Then the LORD spoke to the Judaites through a man named Jahaziel. Jahaziel said, **"The LORD says, 'Do not be afraid or discouraged because of this vast army. For the battle is not yours, but Mine.' "**

Have all JUDAITES including JEHOSHAPHAT say, "Thank You, LORD, for comforting us. What else should we do?"

NARRATOR: Jahaziel told the Judaites what God wanted them to do. The LORD said, "Tomorrow march against your enemies, but you will not have to fight this battle. Take up your positions; stand firm, and the LORD will save you from your enemies because He is with you."

Children remove their belt buckles and lay down their swords. JEHOSHAPHAT and JUDAITES say, "Thank You, LORD, for being with us. We will do as You say." Children remove their breastplates. All the JUDAITES stand.

NARRATOR: As the Judaites prepared to go into battle, Jehoshaphat said, "Listen! **Have faith in the L**ORD **your God, and you will be given strength; have faith in what Jahaziel has told us from the L**ORD**, and we will be successful."** Jehoshaphat had some of the Judaites sing praises to the LORD for His wonderful holiness as they marched to face their enemies.

*JEHOSHAPHAT leads JUDAITES once around the room. All the JUDAITES say repeatedly, "Give thanks to the L*ORD *for His love endures forever."*

NARRATOR: So the people of Judah set out against their enemies, thanking the LORD and worshiping Him. They marched to where their enemies waited without fear or doubt, praising the LORD for His guidance and protection. The LORD caused the enemy soldiers to start fighting among themselves, so they fought one another. All the enemies of the Judaites killed one another even before the Judaite people had reached them.

*JEHOSHAPHAT and JUDAITES stop walking and say, "Praise our L*ORD *God who is always good to us. Look what has happened! Our enemies attacked each other!"*

NARRATOR: Jehoshaphat and the Judaites then returned to Jerusalem, where they went to the temple of the LORD with harps and lutes and trumpets to celebrate the LORD's love for them, and their love for the LORD.

*JEHOSHAPHAT and JUDAITES all say, "Thank You, L*ORD*, for fighting our enemies for us!" Children all return to stand in front of their armor that they laid on the floor.*

NARRATOR: Now look at what you are wearing … you are wearing the armor that Jehoshaphat and the Judaites were wearing when they went to face their enemies … the full armor of God. It is armor we cannot see or touch, but it is what the Judaites wore, and it is something that we wear every day too.

Children pick up their face masks with helmet attachments.

NARRATOR: The Judaites wore a piece of God's armor called the helmet of salvation. There was no doubt in their minds that the Lord loved them, and they were special to Him. Since we believe Jesus is the Son of God and He died on the cross and rose again, we are forgiven for the wrong things we do. Therefore, we can wear the helmet of salvation every day.

Children put on their masks with helmet attachments.

NARRATOR: Jehoshaphat and the Judaites prayed to God and asked Him for His help. God listened to their prayers and told them what they should do. Jehoshaphat and the Judaites believed the Lord would protect them and did as the Lord told them to do. They were wearing the pieces of God's armor called the belt of truth and the sword of the Spirit.

Children pick up their belt buckles and swords.

NARRATOR: We wear those pieces of God's armor too. The belt of truth helps us remain strong in our faith in the Lord. The sword of the Spirit helps us to know what the Lord wants us to do.

Children put on their belt buckles and swords.

NARRATOR: God also gave Jehoshaphat and the Judaites a piece of armor called the breastplate of righteousness. Jehoshaphat and the Judaites not only prayed for the Lord's help and had faith in Him, they also did as the Lord told them.

Children pick up their breastplates.

NARRATOR: The Lord gives us breastplates of righteousness too, to help us make choices that will please God and be good for us.

Children put on their breastplates.

NARRATOR: Sometimes it's hard to remember that God is with us every day because we can't see Him. When we pray for God's protection, He gives us every piece of armor that you're wearing now; we just can't see it. But God sees it. Jehoshaphat and the Judaites weren't wearing armor that they could see and touch when they went to fight their enemies, but they wore the full "invisible" armor of God, and God used that armor to help them.

Now lead children in a march around the room singing the following words to the tune of "Onward, Christian Soldiers."

We believe in Jesus;
He's our shield and might.
Dressed in God's full armor,
We can do what's right.

We can wear God's armor
Each and every day.
He'll protect and help us
When we stop and pray.

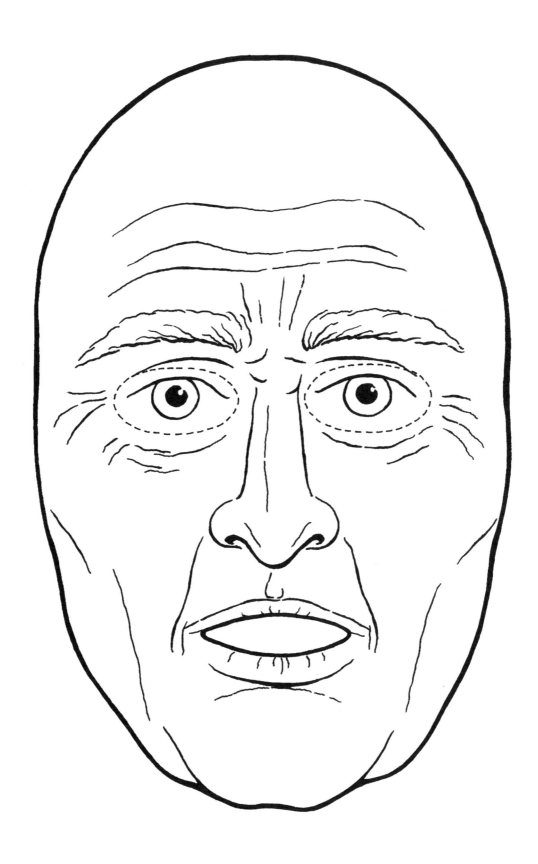

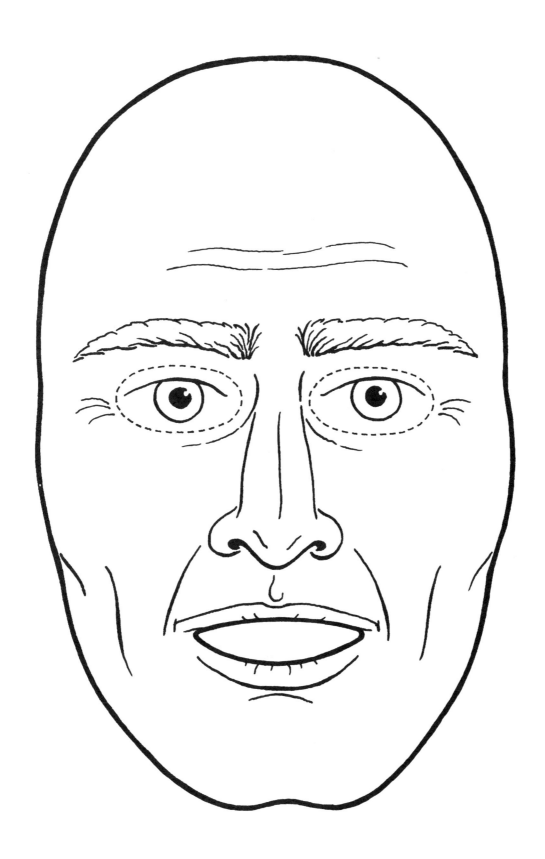

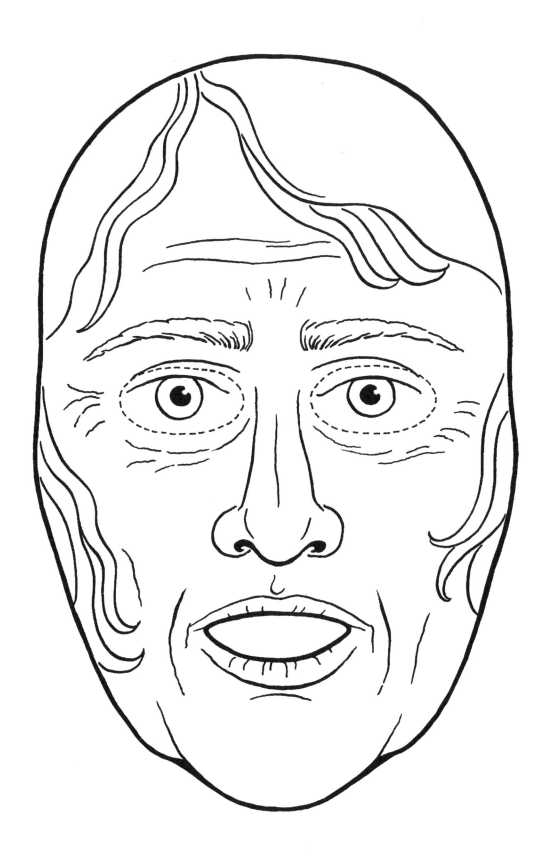

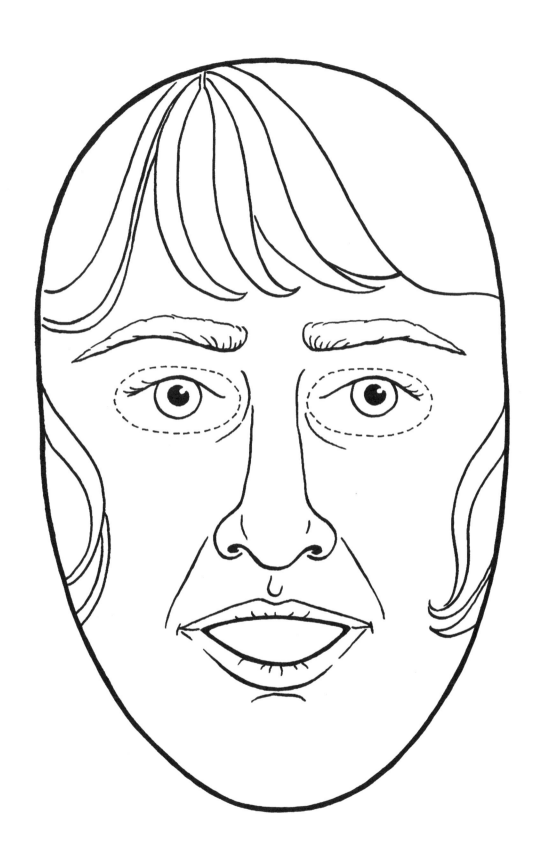

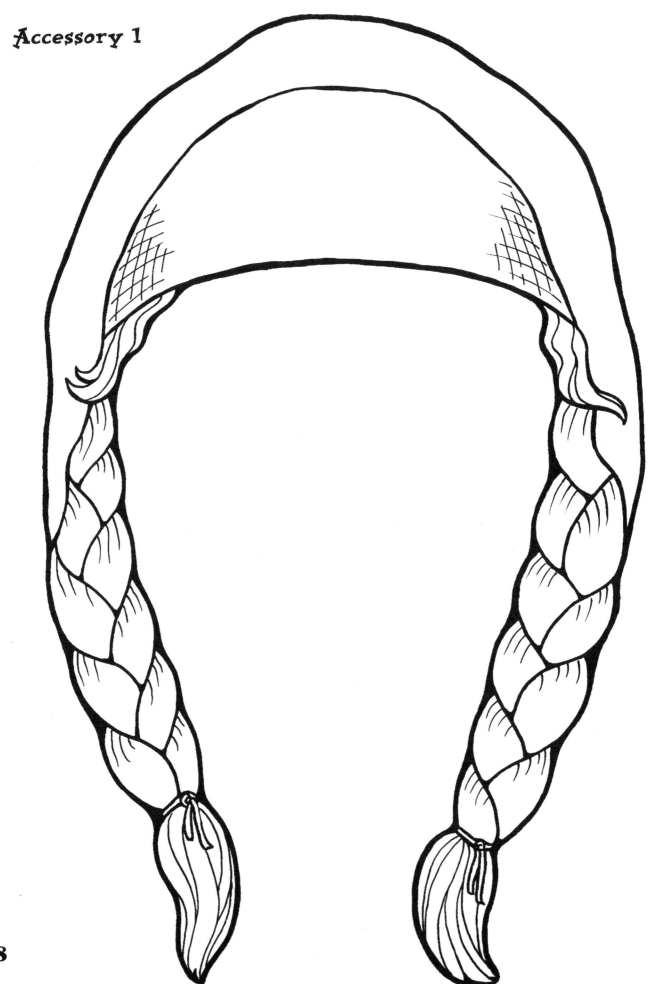

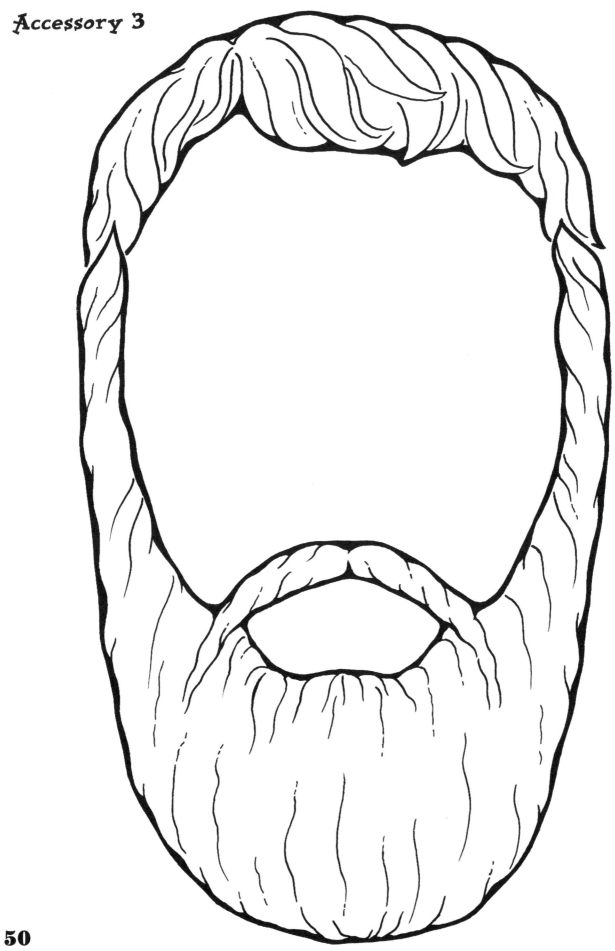

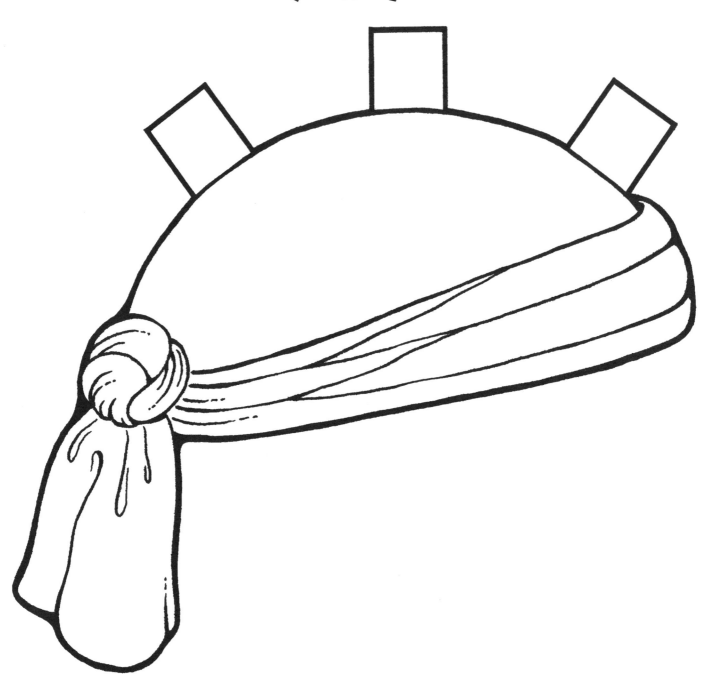

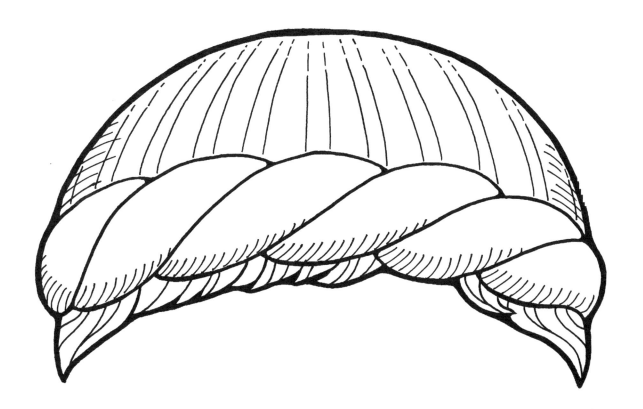

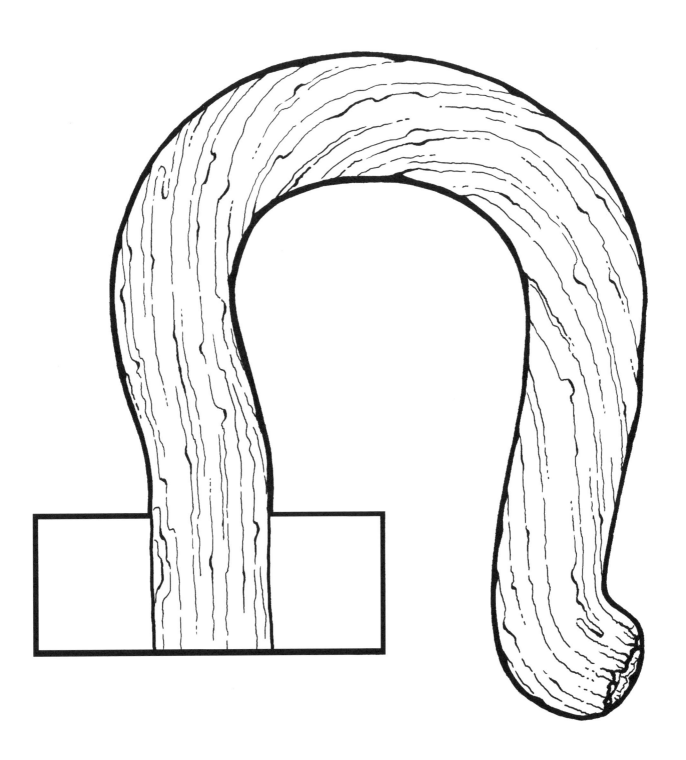

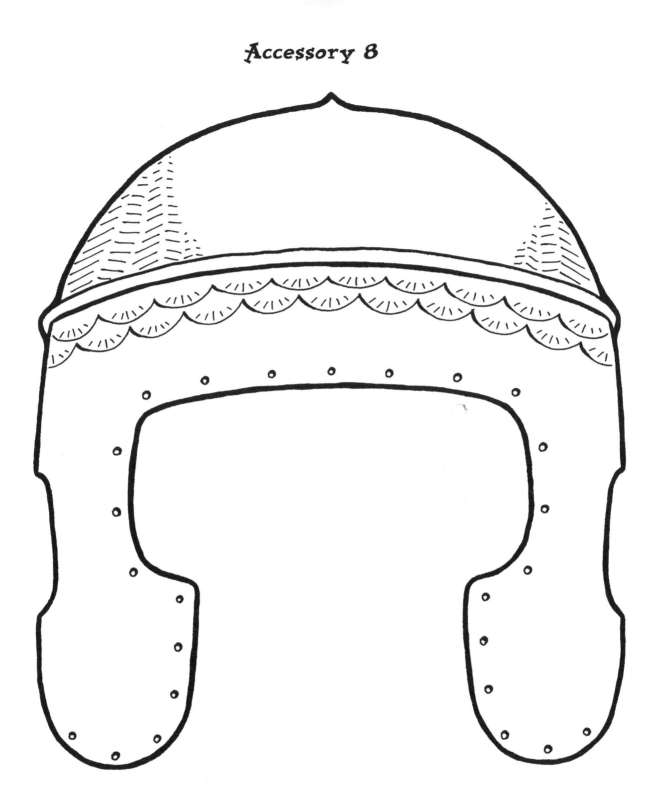

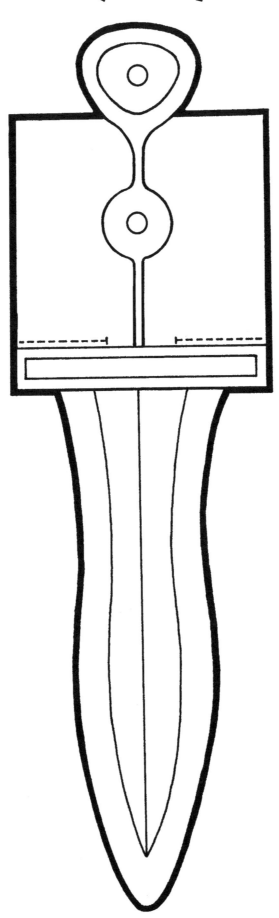

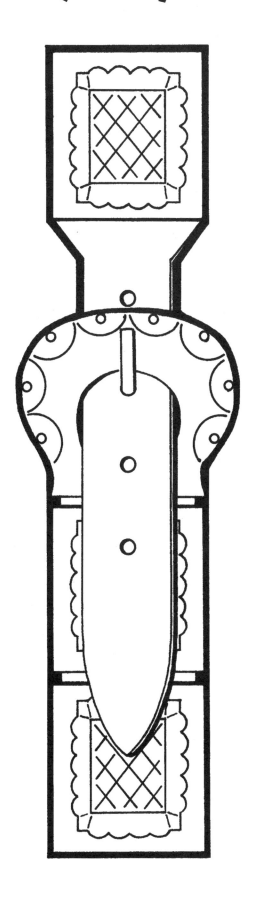

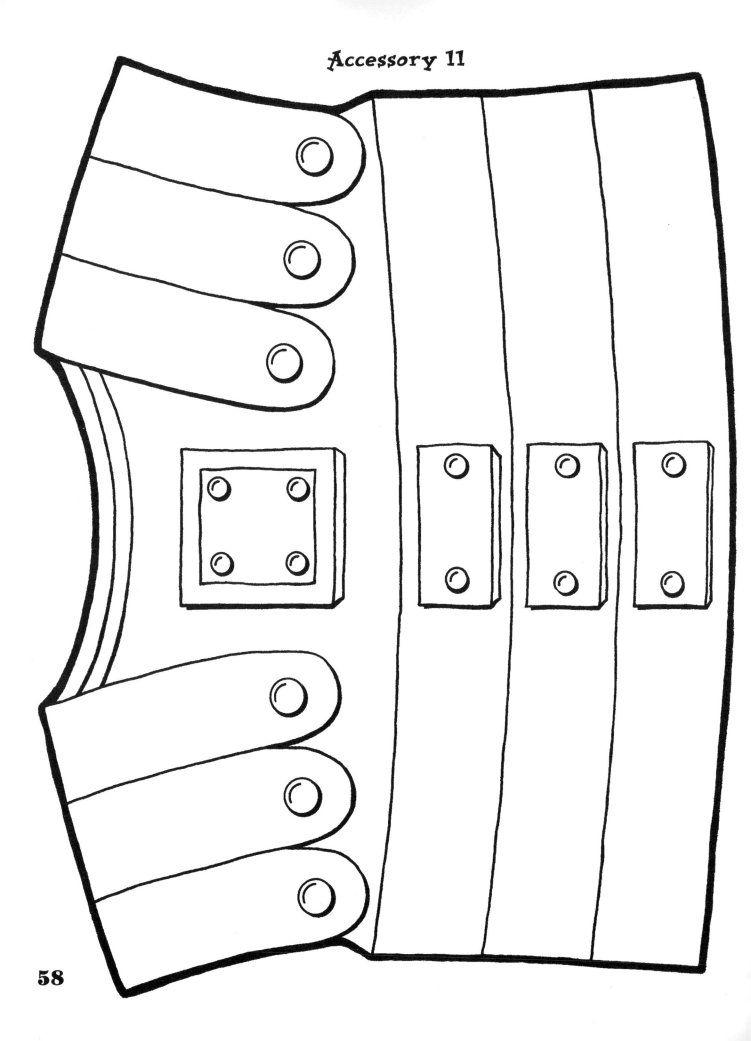

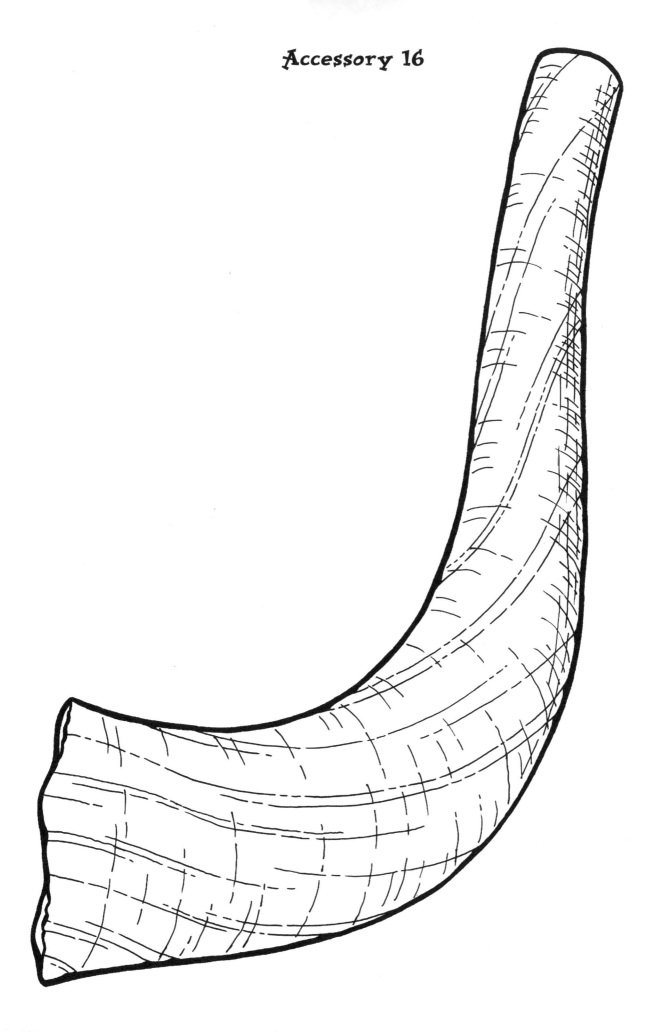

Loaf of Bread, Fish, and Basket

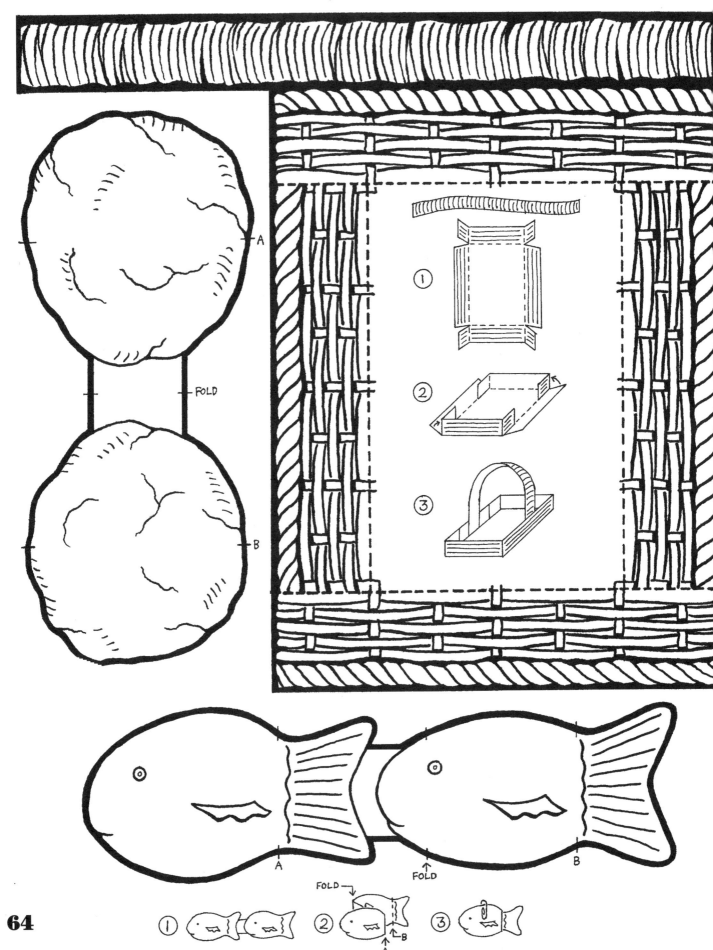

A

FOLD

B

①

②

③

A

FOLD

B

FOLD
A
B

① ② ③